Of What was Love

OrangeBooks Publication

1st Floor, Rajhans Arcade, Mall Road, Kohka, Bhilai, Chhattisgarh 490020
Website: **www.orangebooks.in**

First Edition, 2025

ISBN: 978-93-6554-414-5

Price: Rs. 199.00

Printed in India

OF WHAT WAS LOVE

RUBAL AGRAWAL

OrangeBooks Publication
www.orangebooks.in

Introduction

This book is a piece of my heart, spoken in two languages- Hindi and English.

I did not choose the language for each poem, my feelings chose it for me. I just wrote down the emotions as it flowed. Naturally.

Some verses rose from the earth, warm and rooted, spoken in the soft cadences of Hindi.

Others drifted in like clouds—pensive, sublime, allegorical — in the measured elegance of English.

Hindi carries the warmth of home, a familiar expression of my Heart. English brings clarity, distance, a way to say the unsayable. The way my mind thinks.

Together, they hold the moments I couldn't let go — the love, the ache, the wonder.

I hope, in whatever language you read, you feel something true.

This is not just a collection of poems.

It's a conversation, between my heart and my mind.

Between you and me.

Contents

Prelude to "Of What Was Love......."

Love is never quite lost even when it leaves.

It lingers in the air, in the echoes of words once said,
In glances half remembered, in hands no longer held.

This anthology is a tracing of those echoes and the aftershock of the tender wreckage, the questions left behind when love departs or when it shifts into something unrecognizable.

Of What Was Love is not a story, but a memory. My own lived experience. While I navigate the aftermath through my lyrical ruminations, I do not attempt to offer any answers, only reflections, confessions, and the soft ache of trying to understand **WHY**?

Each poem is a fragment - of the longing, of the loss, of the beauty found in the unravelling, and of the love that's still not lost. Together, they speak of what love was—and, perhaps, what it still will be.

Love, in these pages, is elemental.

It rises as a storm in the heart and condenses into tears. It finds its home in myth, and is expressed as metaphor.

To read this is not to trace a story, but to step into a mood, my mood. To feel the weight of something no longer present yet never quite gone.

तुम्हें पाने का मोह त्याग चुके हैं हम,

और रही बात प्रेम की तो तुमसे आज भी है।

और हमेशा रहेगा, असीमित।

The yearning to possess thee, I have long forsaken,
Yet the love, I hold for thee, remaineth—unshaken.
And aye, it shall endureth past the bounds of time,
Boundless, Infinite, eternal—a love most sublime.

part 1

This isn't a story of end or start,

But love eternal, heart to heart.

So if you've ever loved or cried,

You'll find a part of-me inside.

Each verse a step, rhyme a door,

To heart I've held, the one I store.

Between the sheets, vows and sighs,

Pressed like a rose, that'll never die

1. Tidings of Love

This day we met, six months ago,
Tis' was a lovely day.
U stayed in my arms thro' d night,
And kissed me all the way.
You whispered magic in my ears,
And took my heart away.
With the tidings of love that will be.

Since then life's been heaven,
And love all around.
To live my life each single day,
Eternally bound.
And to hear you say my name,
That magical sound.
That says tidings of love that will be.

I close my eyes and see you,

And feel you in my heart,

No force on earth or heaven,

Can do us ever part,

Oh thank you for being there

And for this new start.

And the tidings of love that will be…

(lines written on 10th Dec, 2023)

2. An Ode to Pyramus and Thisbe

Barred in, by their parents,
Society, men and hoods,
They vowed to meet each other,
In the darkness of the woods.

When the red sun did set,
And night has veiled the pole.
Enrobing herself beautiful,
From home did Thisbe stole.

Stole he also thro' Sleeping town,
Over trip the dewy grass.
To hasten to the darkened woods,
And meet his loving lass.

She walking in dark, dead woods,
Did face a beast with roar.
Dropping her rich, blood stained cloak,
She fled to save her core.

When Pyramus at allotted site,
Saw her cloak on grass.
He thought so base a thought to think,
That beast had killed her lass.

And in grief and out of love,
He stole himself away.
Did, such a cowardly act, to do,
His soul did steal away.

When some hours from hence,
Came Thisbe back at woods.
Seeing her lover lying dead,
Turned mad in limbs and mood.

Thus sadly ends this loving song,
In world, full of sin and hate.
Since ages 'true love never meets'
As destined by the fate.

3. Prophesy

"He'll come at dawn, thro' the dunes,
The hour set, as wrote in runes.
The harvest done and fields ablaze,
That day of solstice in the June."

"Will save you best and killer be,
Shall be the cause of death to thee,"
I tell you truth. And I fore-tell,
The wisest wise, thus spoke to me.

He jumped the sky and bent the light,
Thunder whimpered 'fore his might
His flowing mane, atop the steed,
He rode at cusp of day and night.

He led me, half the earth around,
I followed; nor did make a sound.
To reach, a field of roses red,
And castle build atop a mound.

Days were lovely, sweet and fine,
Dancing, music, drinking wine.
On all earth, what mattered was,
I was HIS; and HE was mine.

We ran together, hand in hand,
In meadows, jungle and in sand,
Till one day, bending on his knees,
He offered me the golden band!

Next day I woke up and I found,
In a lofty tower, I was bound.
Golden band, did chain become,
And he was nowhere to be found.

Chained, bound, hurt, alone.
I, in solitude did mourn,
And, I sought him day and night
Till the count of days was gone

I knew, he would come for me,
Through the fire, across the sea,
Ten autumns came, winters gone,
But never once; did come he!

Crying, on my window sill,
Bore the heat n' suffered the chill.
Till one day, far away I saw,
Another castle on the hill.

The garden grew with roses red,
He walked covered from toe to head,
In silken robes of matching hues,
With person, whom he fondly led!

I watched the castle day and night,
Cursed my fate, mourned my plight.
Till one day, I woke up to see,
The castle gone. New tower in sight.

That moment things, changed around
Robes replaced my shoddy gown.
My chains were gone and tears dried,
Lofty tow'r came crashing down.

Still sometime in sleep I see,
His outstretched arms, holding me.
His lips murmuring a lovely song
Of promises of love and WE.

But now I know, It was a dream,
A Magic weave of shine and gleam,
But my love, for him was pure.
Like ever flowing mountain stream.

They yet often that story tell,
Of how HE lives in a tower cell,
trapped by his own magic weave.
But the wisest one, did foretell.

4. Who Needs Forever

Whoever loveth, that loveth not at the first sight,
What love did not give lover, the sleepless night.
The course of my love too, shall never run smooth.
Will devour my heart, feed on the soul of my youth.

And above my head, I can hear the music in the air,
I believe there is a heaven, with him somewhere.
It's love; no rules. And this time I won't play it fair,
There is nothing for his sake, on earth I won't dare.

The path is daunting, and the going will be rough,
I've loved with all my heart, and that to me is enough.
love this real, love this fierce, shall never cease to be.
I love, cause not loving him, will be impossible for me.

Whatever the souls are made of, his is same as me,
If I perished, and he remained, I should continue to be.
Certainty this strong, happens only once in a lifetime,
And who needs forever; when in mortal life he's mine.

5. Is it Love?

Is it the same sun, burning bright?
No shadows, of dark yesternight.
Aren't the birds more loud and gay,
Darting like arrows of the light.

The stream flows clear, the sky seems near,
The swallows sing, Oh! Don't you hear?

Rose smells sweeter, than yesterday,
A cooler wind doth blow from bay,
There seems to be a music in the air,
To which the Trees, dance & sway.

The sand and the Sea, the day to be
It all seems new. Is it love or it's just me"?

6. Perspective

i.

Ever watched a candle at the night,
flickering but still burning bright.
It's for you, that I know is true.
While they see the light and smile,
the candle actually burns for you.

ii.

"You will burn" they said and burn alone and end it be.
What if I burn? I will light his life don't you see!

7. Singing in the Shower

Singing in the shower,
and Laughing by the hour,
oh! how much I love this game.

Kisses on my lips,
Your gentle finger tips,
I really love to hear u say my name.

The river running by,
And sunset in the sky,
No wonder, it's a perfect scene.

Sitting by your side,
In your arms I hide,
Live is like a perfect dream.

I like your eyes and your smile,

Walking, with you for miles.

Baby do u really know what I mean?

I just love being with you.

8. On Leaving

My bags are packed, and sail is set,
and I shall leave sharp at dawn,
To brave the rough seas out there,
Alone, while you shall stay on.

I leave all my shadows behind,
To cover you while the sun is bright,
I leave my hug to warm your heart,
On a cold deserted winter night.

While I alone shall, rough sea brave,
To reach towards my journey's end.
I pray you have a peaceful night,
My love to thee, I shall send.

At sunset, when my heart is weak,
And breathe remaining with me few.
Even then, my every thought,
My only prayers shall be you.

9. I Shall Die

Every day I have died waiting for you,
alone in the sleepless dark night,
When all around was calm and quiet,
I have, but heard my heart cry.
I have not, but I shall die, one day
while you are far away.

10. When I am no More

How shall u know when I am not here,
But how? How will you know it my dear?
At every sunset, 'n at every dawn
Will you know it, when I am gone?
Who shall, but who, just in case.
Die, to only look at your face?

Who shall, but take those walks,
Of spoken words and silent talks.
Oh! who shall wait for you in vain,
Alone, on sleepless nights in rain.

Sun shall shine 'n winds will blow,
Even if today, I decide to go,
But who will hold that shade to you
And feed you on the morning dew?

My words scribbled on empty page,
Shall make it the perfect image.
No wind shall dare blow harshly o'er
Even when, I am no more…….!

11. Nothing Gold Can Ever Stay

It's always hard to say goodbye,
Especially tough, tonight for me.
But for anything on this earth,
I would've always chosen thee.

It's better to have loved and lost
Then never to have loved at all.
I feel that, when I sorrow most.
And hold true, whatever befall.

To let go love, is not that easy,
I'll let it sink, as dawn does day.
You are the apple of my eye,
But nothing gold can ever stay.

12. Thousand Years of Wait

You left me and moved ahead,
But you will come back, you've said.
I'll wait till the end of the night
With you shall dawn my day, my light.
Till then, I promises shall hold,
And do it all as you have told,
My every breath, my beat shall be,
Waiting for you to be with me.
You have forgotten, but not me,
My memories shall make you see,
Have waited already for thousand years,
Have felt the loss n'cried those tears,
Will wait again for thousand more,
Just to make you mine for sure,

I'll never let you cry again
Have cried for both and borne the pain
A moment in your close embrace,
Is worth thousand years of wait,
Nothing in world I wouldn't do,
Just for one moment with you,
Come back soon, don't be so late,
That mortal life does end my wait,

13. 1201

Today. whatever the faith decree,
This day be kept in joy by me!
This day then let you not be told,
You add an year and you grow old.
Nor you must think of future ills,
Of growing old and popping pills.
But to thee, this promise I make,
I'll never leave you, for heaven's sake.
When we are old, bend and week,
With a whisper, trailing voice we speak.
Then from reason, may be brought,
A better, more pleasing thought,
Of days and talks of younger past.
Of laughs and joys that will last,

Which can, in spite of all decays,
See you through your ageing days.
When sipping coffee, we do wait,
To cut your 90th birthday cake!
To that day, be with you and say,
My bestie you were born this Day!

(Lines written on 1st Dec, 2023)

14. That's My Only Wish Today

It's here now, good time to say,
Bestie you were born this day.
As you cut your birthday cake,
No new promises, I would make.
May not be there, around and all,
But there to catch you, if you fall.
Been watching you from far away,
I pray for your best, every day.
Life's got some other plans for us,
No point creating, any more fuss.
If in future, we meet some day,
I may not have the courage to say,
"Let's do a "Tea" for old times' sake"
That, I know would be a big mistake.

This day and this moment right,
Is all I have, and I cannot fight,
The past. We must leave behind.
And future, I shall pray be Kind.
May love lighten your life's way,
And that's my only wish today.

(lines written on 24th Dec,2024)

15. I Set You Free

Love liberates and does not bind.
I understand and no, I don't mind.
You need Permission to Go? and I,
Set you free. Go. Fly. find your Sky.

I love you, this love shall never end,
For you, my prayers I'll always send.
I love you, when you are around me,
And I love, when you, I can't even see.

I would've loved, to be in your arms,
To Look in your eyes, feel the charm.
To take the walk, on a moonlit night,
Hand in hand. Oh, what a delight!

But it is not a possibility. Not now,
I know this truth, but somehow,
It does not bother me anymore. And I
Set you free. Go. Fly. Find your Sky.

I'll still love you when you are gone,
From sun to moon and dusk to dawn.
Leaving expectations, task I take on me,
Live your life. Go. I set you free.

16. How I wish, I were...

Oh, how I wish I were a fish,
In some small alpine stream,
In crystal waters I would swim,
With silver fins and golden gleam.

I would love, too, to be a cloud,
Vast and white against the sky,
And drift along on summer winds,
While all below would watch me fly.

Or better still, if I were a rose,
Of scarlet red, a lovely hue,
Some maiden with her tender lips
Would kiss my petals, wet with dew.

Or better still, I were a breeze,
That stirs the hair of one I love,
A breath of warmth upon his skin,
A gift of longing, from above.

Or sweetest yet, I'd be a flame,
A fire in my lover's eyes,
To warm the nights with secret dreams
And set ablaze the longing skies.

Or maybe I could be a song,
A whispered tune, from his lips,
To dance upon his gentle breath,
And linger sweet on fingertips.

What if I could be a dream,
I'd kiss his lips in silent gleam,
And leave my love upon his soul,
To linger past the morning's beam.

How I wish I were the moon,
To watch him from the skies above,
To kiss his night with silver hue.
And guard and cradle him with love.

But most of all, I'd wish to be,
A heartbeat pressed against his own,
To live and linger in his chest,
And never face the dark alone.

And if no more, than this I be
A breath, a kiss, a fleeting gleam,
I'd count it joy,to love him so,
Beyond the stars, beyond the dream.

17. I Shall Let You Go

I am not moving on, but I shall let you go
Will I ever stop loving you? the answer is No.
We may not talk, but always remember,
I will always be there, and that you know.

It's hard and I don't deny I won't miss you,
It hurts, but I know not, what else to do.
I yearn to speak, meet and give you a hug
I want that. But my place, I know that too.

We may not talk, but you are on my mind,
And love, I have learned, does not bind.
I have to focus, and let my own heart heal,
Accept you're gone, and to myself be kind.

It was not meant to be, and it never will be,
'Twas simple, but my love made me not see.
I can't force love, nor can I prove my worth,
Love happens and it just happened to me.

18. The Way I Love You

Is to moon and back, the way I love you?
Or I love you, like bees to the flowers do?
Or shall I say, I love thee with every breath,
That I take; and will love you till my death.
I love you under the sun and in the night,
And love you in the wrong, love you in right.
I love you as free, as a child does play,
With pure Joy, like the sky on a sunny day.
I love you, with the might of a thunderstorm,
and of crashing waves. And I defy the norm,
By loving you in a thousand ways and more,
Each greater than the last. And I am sure,
I love you cause I don't know, how not to.
Unloving you, is what I cannot ever do.

19. Scrap Book

What memories do I save of you?
Quiet talks, resounding through the noises
of the distant past, a few cheerful tears,
and some painful smiles, ever fading into
the thickening mist of the yester-years.
Few smiles, some leaps and plenty of falls.
And a leaf picked up, from the tree,
that saw me metamorphose and fly, free.
into the unpleasant world of "pleasant
maturity". And a rose, gathered from inside
the door, that I cannot now ever enter!
Hope you too have saved my smile.
The only place I think I can find it now.
It takes so little space in your scrap book.

20. The Journey Alone

Tears roll down, as the river draws near.
I can see the temple flag; the chats I hear.
I travel this road all alone; one more time.
For our sake, though the journey was not mine,
To travel alone. I am weary and old.
My heart, already breaking from the weight
of my dead love, has grown heavy and cold.
Hope the mind holds Strong. Forgetting never
has been my best skill. No, It has not ever.
It is already starting to resemble a graveyard.
Broken and overgrown with memories old
These are the times, I for a poor memory pray.
My heart is stagnant and frail, and emotions lay
Bare, stuck in the Quagmire of the wilted love.

(Lines written on 9th June, 2024, while on way to Alandi)

21. My love is Infinite.

It feels strange. But no l am not lonely.
But this distant feeling that I have got.
Of missing something. That Something,
which was supposed to be, but is not.
As I glaze out of the aircraft's window,
I see a stretch of an endless sky. Blue.
For miles, freckled with small formless
clouds. Clouds of every shape and hue.
The mind plays tricks and the clouds
don't seem fun either. Shapeless heaps.
With no purpose, just like life. Or is it?
Patches of happiness strewn in leaps,
across the decades of life, that stretches
aimlessly all around me, just like the sky
outside my window. An endless infinity.
But some infinities are larger than other
Infinities. Just like my Love was.
And will be Infinite Unbound, forever.

22. I Become Nothing

I will become whatever you want me to.
A promise I made to you.
I burned myself into a fire, when it was cold around,
I melted into water, when your thirst you found,
I hardened into stone, to keep you firm and sound
And I was the air, invisible but always around.
But then you wanted a toy to play,
I become one for you, so you would stay.
You got bored. You wanted the toy no more.
You wanted Nothing. I had made a promise.
I kept my promise, and I turned into NOTHING for you.

23. The Poisoned Cup

I carried the burden of my broken heart.
Wearing the grief like my second skin,
Till it seeped into me, and became one,
With my soul. I forgot, how it wasn't done.
I walked through memories, searching you,
And the promised love, in my dreams
Where your love, like a mirage shone.
And kept me alive while destroying me.
Parched and thirsty to my bare bone,
I Begged for a drink, from the sweet
alluring forbidden stream. I begged thee.
You smiled, and offered me that cup.
I grabbed and Drank the nectar of love,
till my limbs felt numb, the poisoned cup.
Crawling at your feet, feeble, I lay bare.

I looked at you, while u sat there.

I knew, drinking it will kill me. I died.

And I died for love, But it saved me too;

It took me years to gather my dead,

into a bundle, shoved beneath my bed.

"It's time to bury the non-living, and go on"

They say it's the only way of life of forlorn.

What else is there to do! What else?

But to live, and go on!

24. I Do Not Conform

Moving on is different for different people,
And May be, I will never be able to move on.
Cause I know not how to unlove and be gone,
From a person's life, who I loved so much.
But maybe I am different. I don't conform.

Never had begged in my life for anything
but I cried, begged and pleaded that day.
Let's work it out, we sure will find a way.
You denied and left, and never looked back
But Maybe I am different, I chose to stay.

I miss that voice. That one smile, which
I will still give my life to see. But it's fine.
I have accepted, you are no more mine,
But you gave me my forever. And that shall
like a beckon, through my dark days shine.

25. Love That Was and Ever Will Be

In shadows soft where memories lie,
Beneath the hush of twilight sky,
There burns a flame no time can still—
A love that was, and lingers still.

It bloomed before the world began,
In silent dreams of sculpted sand,
Through lifetimes lost and yet to come,
Its whispered name forever sung.

It lives in me; with me to grave,
It braves the tide and rides the wave.
Though faces fade and voices trail
The love remains, it will not fail.

No chain no clock can bind its grace,
It lives in every time and place.
Beyond the stars, beneath the sea—
Love that was and ever will be.

26. View from an Aeroplane Window

Some journeys are meant to be taken alone.
Today is one such day when I will have to,
Bear it all alone. And yes I shall.
It hurts, it pains, and always Will.
As the plane ascends and I look down,
Life seems good, from a distance.
I wonder, if that's the way to live life,
From a distance. Never getting too close,
Never getting too involved. May be.
I can see the fields, small houses,
the river, the dark clouds and the rains,
without getting wet. But is that any fun?
I see men trapped in the cycle of living,
Walking down the well laid paths,

That cuts across the emerald fields,
around the woods, and houses
And over a small narrow bridge
over the River, that wriggles like an eel.
Shimmering. It all seems like a set up.
A trap, with Beauties thrown in,
to prevent escape. Yes, it seems so like Life.
Yet the sun shines like hope,
but it shall set in before,
I touch the ground again.
What a poetic resemblance to my life.

27. Do They Dream in Death?

When death finally finds me hiding,
Under the shadows of your love. I hope,
It whispers, "come your fight is over.
I hope it holds my hands firm, and looks
at me like an old friend would, and say.
"I understand why you are so tired.
Rest, let me, share your burned now.
You need not worry ever again."
I hope it hugs me like my lover, and Say,
"You have borne enough. Let me bear this,
for you now. Close your eyes and sleep."
And spreads its arms, wide to hug.
And I hope I find peace the moment, I
snug in that embrace, like I would have
in my lovers arms. And holding me tight,
I hope the death lulls me to sleep.
I want to know if they dream in death?

28. Love.... I hold With Pride

I loved you with my heart and soul,
A feeling that was pure and whole.
Your laughter lit the darkest skies,
A spark of joy behind your eyes.

We built a world with tender hands,
Dreamed of far and distant lands.
In every breath, I felt you near,
Your voice, the song I longed to hear.

But seasons change, and so did you,
Like Sun does to the morning dew.
The warmth I knew began to fade,
And love grew quiet, in the shade.

You drifted where I could not go,
silence, where your words would flow.
I held on tight, you let me fall—
Now shadows echo through it all.

A thousand nights, I searched in vain,
For pieces of you, in the rain.
Deep within this broken chest,
Your memories still, refuse to rest.

Though torn apart by time and fate,
What once we had, I won't negate.
For even sorrow, deep and wide,
Was born from love I hold with pride.

29. An Ode to love

It blooms in silence, shines in rain,
It soothes sorrow, sweetens pain.
lingers in laughter, hides in tears
Stretches across the days and years

It's light in dark, the song in sigh,
Reason we dream, reason we try.
Through storm and sorrow, loss and fear,
Thy steadfast music we shall hear.

O Love thou speak, when lips are still,
That bends, but breaks not to the will,
Thou art the breath, we cannot see,
Yet live and move and hope in Thee

Thou walketh through darkest night,
A flame unseen, yet burning bright.
Thou lift the low, the lost, the weak,
And give the silent heart its speak.

Beyond all sorrow, grief, and pain,
Thou rises pure, and fall like rain,
A holy song, both brave and wise,
O Love, O Love, that never dies.

30. I lost Myself

I lost me, while losing you.
Pieces of me, now remain few.
Broken, tired I gave up the fight,
But I never gave up on you!

I forgive you and nothing is due,
We had a future, me and you.
You broke me over a 1000 times,
But I never gave up on you.

I don't have it in me, now to try,
It hurts, it pains and I still cry,
Muffled in pillow, my tears flow,
Silently, as the world goes by.

31. I'll Love You Still-But Silently

The price of love, I paid with grace
Though every tear, did leave a trace.
My heart, my soul, each whispered plea,
All cast away, for what could be!

I bore the weight of every lie,
Wrapped in words both soft and sly.
I knew thy craft, thy sweet disguise
Yet hoped one day you'll read my eyes.

The lies you wove, the truth you stole,
Left scars upon my wounded soul.
You had my trust, yet you betrayed,
In every silence, a price I paid.

My soul was Price, I had to pay.
To have you close and make you stay.
But love that's forced will never do,
And I was never 'nough for you.

I broke in silence, cracked in light,
Held on through every sleepless night.
You were a storm, I had to pass,
To see myself in a cleaner glass.

Now when I walk, I walk alone,
But not as one who's lost or lone.
I rise from all you tore apart,
With clearer eyes and stronger heart.

I paid the price and no regrets,
No chain remains and no old debts,
From far afar, where I walk free...
I'll love you still- but silently.

32. Why don't I hate?

Why don't you hate him, they ask,
After all that he's done to you.
But why must it breed poison?
Must scars carry a grudge too?

He hurt me, yes—but I loved him.
And That part won't give way.
Love doesn't end, with the ending.
Some hearts choose to stay.

My love was not the perfect love
And I won't pretend, all was right.
But my love wasn't only for sun,
it lived through the darkest night.

So no, I don't hate him, I can't
Not a story I want to tell.
I choose to cherish the lovely time,
And let the rest sit where it fell.

33. Reverie

1

There are nights, when the silence is deafening.
The only noise is of my heart breaking under the burden of love.
My mind screaming questions. Answers to which I will never have.
Was it all a dream? No it could not have been.
The pain is too real.

2

I look in the mirror, to find a stranger looking back.
Plastered with a fake smile, that's not even set as deep as wrinkles.
I look through the eyes, to see them swell with tears.
Full of hope.
But the heart knows, the hope is false. Just like the image in the mirror. One can see, but never have it.

3

I still find myself standing at the edge of the memories
we created together.
Reliving the moments and reaffirming the promises,
you failed to keep.
I sometimes wonder, if they meant anything to you?
Cause if they did, would you have left as you did?

4

While trying to gather the pieces of me, you left behind,
I still gasp, through the pain of your absence.
I was the only one fighting for us then, fighting to stay.
I am the only one fighting now. Fighting the pain,
Fighting the loneliness.
Alone.

5

I gave you the most fragile parts of me- my love,
my hope
and my future.
But you walked away, like none of this ever mattered.
My love was all yours. But you took away my dreams.
And that was the worst part. I don't dream any more.
I am scared lose them again.

6

Our story ended long ago. But this won't be the end of my story.

I am ready to fly again, even if it means I have to start by crawling.

I am ready to live. Love though won't happen again.

And that's Life. We move on.

There is, but no other option.

34. An Ode to my broken heart

O faithful heart, so fierce, so wide,
Thou dared to love, then bled with pride.
Thou held thy world within thy beat,
And shattered yet, remain'th complete.

Thou bore the weight of silent cries,
Of promises turned naught but lies.
Thou sang'st in joy, then broke in pain,
Yet found'st the strength to love again.

Each cry, a map of where thou'st been,
Of battles lost, and love within.
Thou art, not weak for all thy scars,
But braver still for where you are.

Thou taught the soul how deep it feels,
How time won't rush, what time must heal.
Though torn apart and slow to mend,
Thou pulse with hope that will not end.

O heart, my heart, so bruised and torn,
Thy courage shines, though thou dost mourn.
In every fall, thy strength is shown,
For Love, unbroken, stands alone.

part 2

प्रेम यदि राधा है, तो प्रेम मीरा भी है। मीरा का प्रेम मात्र भक्ति नहीं -आत्मा की पुकार थी, जो श्रीकृष्ण में पूर्णता खोजती थी। उसी अद्वितीय भावभूमि पर खड़ी हैं ये अगली कविताएँ। इन गीतों में पीर है— विरह की, प्रतीक्षा की, और आत्मविसर्जन की।

आइए, इन कविताओं के माध्यम से उस प्रेम को अनुभूत करें जो समाज की सीमाओं, रिश्तों की परिभाषाओं और समय की बेड़ियों से परे है— अखंड, अमूर्त, और शाश्वत।

1. सुन लीजो अरज ये म्हारी

श्री सुन लीजो अरज ये म्हारी,
स्व कर में बन बाँसुरिया, मैं होठ को चूमूँ तिहारी।

चंदन बन, श्री ललाट पे चमकूँ, पल पल जाऊँ बलिहारी।
रजत की पैजनिया बन खनकूँ, जब पग धरे बनवारी!

मोर मुकुट की पंखूरीया, सिर सोहूं बाँके बिहारी!
श्री चरणों की रज मस्तक, मोरा, प्रीतम तू गिरधारी।

2. श्री संग होली

होरी के दिन रंग रंग को,
श्री को प्रेम अबीर उड़ो है।
लाल रंग में रंग दे साँवरिया
वा से श्री को मोह जुड़ो है!

स्याह रंग से तन को रंगा के
लागे कारो श्याम खड़ो है।
केसरिया की चमक निराली,
श्री काँधे पे शालो धरो है!

मोर मुकुट सो रंग रंगीलो,
नील-हरो सब रंग पड़ो है!
पीले रंग की छींट लगे सो,
कानन कुंडल रतन जड़ो है!

रंग श्वेत जो श्रीधर धारें,
अबरक चारो ओर पड़ो है!
होरी में मोहे रंग दे साँवरिया
श्री को प्रेम अबीर उड़ो है!

बरसाने में खेलूँ होरी
वा पे राधा रास करो है!
वृंदा वन में खेलूँ होरी,
हिरदय में जे आस धरो है।

होरी में मोहे रंग दे साँवरिया,
श्री को प्रेम अबीर उड़ो है।
होरी के रंग फीके लागे
श्री के प्रेम का रंग चढ़ो है!

3. श्री

श्री, धर राधिका की चुनरी, चिढ़ाते उन्हें
गोपी संग तट पर करैं हैं अठखेलियाँ।
राधा धमकाती, उन्हें अखियाँ दिखा डराती
हास परिहास करें राधा की सहेलियाँ।

श्री, हर चीर छुपाते ऊँची डालियो पे,
भीगी, खिसियानी खड़ी, जमुना के पानी से।
कसमे धराती गोपी, दे दो श्याम कपड़े,
कान्हा को मनाओ, बोलें वो भी राधा रानी से।

श्रीहरि नटखट, जमुना के तट पर,
रास रचाते कान्हा गोपियों के संग में।
गोकुल की ग्वालिने, राधा रानी ब्रज की,
रंग गए सब मन श्याम जी के रंग में।

श्री, धर कर में, लकुटिया घुमत फिरे,
गोप ग्वाल संग मिल, गाऊए चराते हरि।
छल से अबल की मटकी भी फोर देते,
सखा संग छिके चढ़ा माखन चुराते हरि।

4. श्री दर्शन को तरसत अँखियाँ

श्री दर्शन को तरसत अँखियाँ,
बरसत नयनन धार रे।
चरण कमल की चाहत लागी,
बिनु देखे भी प्यार रे।

तन अर्पण, मोरा मन भी अर्पित,
नाम जपूँ दिन-रात रे।
जाने कब मिलें मोसे सांवरिया,
सूनी है मोरी बाट रे।

भीतर जलती विरह की अग्नि,
छूटे न अब यह भार रे।
एक दरस तो श्री दिखला दो,
कट जाए संसार रे।

तन मन सुध बुध बिसर गई सब,
रह गई तुझ से प्रीत रे।
चरण कमल में छाँव मिले तो,
पूरी हो जाए रीत रे।

बिनु श्री मन को चैन न आवे,
दिल है व्याकुल, हार रे।
श्री दर्शन को तरसत अँखियाँ,
बरसत नयनन धार रे।

5. अधूरे गीत

1

कई रातों का जागा हूँ, मगर मैं सो नहीं सकता,
तेरी खाई हुई कसमों के कारण रो नहीं सकता,
दिल ही दिल में तुझसे प्यार इतना आज करता हूँ,
मैं तेरा हूँ नहीं फिर भी, किसी का हो नहीं सकता।

2

मेरे सुखे दरख़्तों पे तेरी यादों का साया है,
जो माटी सीच सकता था, वह सावन आज आया है,
उसकी की राह तकते, ज़िन्दगी ने साथ छोड़ा है,
जो ज़िंदा देखता न था, मेरे मरने पे आया है।

3

तू जाता है तो जाने दे, तेरे ख़्वाबों में रह लेंगे,
वफ़ा कर बेवफ़ा होने के ताने सुन के सह लेंगे,
तेरे से क्या करूँ शिकवे, शिकायत, तू नहीं मेरा,
ख़ुद ही की बात सुन लेंगे, ख़ुद ही से दर्द कह लेंगे।

4

तू मेरा चाँद है, सूरज है, तू मेरा ही सितारा है,
मेरी अंधियारी रातों का, तू जगनू एक प्यारा है,
तेरे होने से हर मुश्किल मुझे आसान लगती है,
तू कश्ती है, तू ही साहिल, तू लहरों का किनारा है।

5

तुझी से दिन निकलता है, तुझी से रात होती है,
तुझी हो शुरू, तुझपे, ख़त्म हर बात होती है,
बहुत कोशिश करी तुझको मेरे दिल से भूलाने की,
मगर फिर भी मेरी हर शय में तेरी बात होती है।

6

तेरे जीते से मैं जीता, तेरे हारे से मैं हारा,
तेरे रहने से रहता है, मेरा आबाद जग सारा,
अकेले ही लड़ा हूँ मैं, ज़माने की कतारों से,
मेरा तो दर्द इतना है, मुझे अपनों ने ही मारा।

7

मेरे टूटे हुए दिल की, अधूरी ये कहानी है,
हंसी झूठी है चेहरे पे, मगर आँखों में पानी है,
अकेला ही बहा हूँ मैं मोहब्बत के समंदर में,
ना कश्ती है, ना साहिल है, ना मौजों में रवानी है।

8

मुझे मारा, मगर मरने का तू इल्जाम दे देना,
वो रुखी सी मुलाकातें, वो सुनी शाम दे देना,
कोई भी दाग न आये कभी मेरे समान तुझ पर,
ज़िकर जब बेवफा का हो, तो मेरा नाम ले लेना।

9

मेरे ऐ-दोस्त, तू मेरा आख़िरी ये काम कर देना,
सभी किस्से शिकायत के, तू मेरे नाम कर देना,
कोई पूछे तो कह देना कि मैं ही बेवफा निकला,
तू उसको पाक रख कर के, मुझे बदनाम कर देना।

10

कभी टूटा कभी हारा, मगर मैं कह नहीं पाया,
ज़माने की रवायत में, कभी भी बह नहीं पाया,
अधूरी रह गई मेरी कहानी, प्यार के किस्से,
कभी तू सुन नहीं पाया, कभी मैं कह नहीं पाया

11

वो दिल के घाव पे मरहम लगा के सी नहीं पाए,
तेरी चाहत में मरना था, मगर हम जी नहीं पाए,
तेरी महफ़िल में रुस्वा दिल के आंसू खूब टपके हैं,
जो साकी ने थमाया जाम, उसे हम पी नहीं पाए।

६. वो गुज़रा ज़माना।

मुझे याद है आज भी वो गुज़रा ज़माना।
मुझे याद है वो मिलने का हर एक बहाना।
मिलना रोज़ रोज़ का,मेरे पास ही आना।
वो मिलना लंच ब्रेक में, मेरे हाथ से खाना!
वो कॉल सुबह की, तेरा वो डी पी लगाना,
क्लास में वो छुप के सब से फोन घुमाना।
लड़ना-झगड़ना, पलट के आँख दिखाना।
वो रूठना तेरा, वो मेरा प्यार जताना।
वो देखना तेरा दूर से, और होंठ दबाना,
वो हँसना तेरा प्यार से, और मेरा मर जाना।

7. कभी शाम को मिलने आना।

मोहब्बत में अगर कुछ दे सको तो वक्त देना,
बिना मतलब के मिलना, और हथेली चूम लेना।
मेरे गालों को छूकर, प्यार से हसना हसाना,
कभी गर वक्त हो तो शाम को मिलने आना।

चलेंगे साथ में उस टपरी पे, वही चाय पियेंगे,
पुराने उस समय को याद कर वो पल जियेंगे।
कुछ हम कहेंगे, कुछ बातें तुम अपनी सुनना,
कभी गर वक्त हो तो शाम को मिलने आना।

8. माँ बस अब और नहीं

वो जून की दोपहरी और माँ का पंखा झलना,
अपने हिस्से की सूखी रोटी पर घी का मलना।
रख देना मेरी थाली में, कहती उसे भूक नहीं थी
पूरे घर का बोझ, तुलसी आँगन की सूख रही थी
सालो पहले, लाल सारी में, आई थी अपने घर से,
आज तक लाज का पल्लू भी ना सरका सर से,

पापा की पुरानी शर्ट से, अपना साया थी सिलती,
घरखर्च, दादी की दवाई, छोटू की फ़ीस भी मिलती,
उसके संदूक में रक्खे, बाँधे एक रेशमी रूमाल में,
सालों गुज़ार दिए उसने, इस गृहस्थी के ख्याल में।
बुआ की शादी, घर का बटवारा, पर वह खड़ी रही,
विषम परिस्थिति, पर कर्तव्य पर अपने आड़ी रही,

वही पुरानी अलमारी, एक चारपाई और संदूक,
सब लुटा के भी यही मिला, कहाँ हो गई चूक?
धुंधली पड़ी एल्बम में संजोये थे उसने कुछ सपने,
एक छोटा सा घर अपना,और साथ में सारे अपने।
अब मुंबई में बसा हूँ, पर फ़सा हूँ उस दोपहर में
बुलाया बहुत पर वह आई नहीं कभी इस शहर में।

बच्चो के कहने पे, अम्मा आ जाती है कभी कभार
पर यहाँ आना, रहना, लगता उनको बच्चो पे भार।
इतनी महंगाई में, कैसे बेटे का घर चलता होगा?
उस पर मेरा खर्चा भी उसी वेतन से करता होगा।
कमर दुखती, पर कहती नहीं.महँगी दवाई के डर से,
और पैसे बच जाए, तो राशन ले आती गाँव के घर से।

फ्लैट, गाड़ी, फुल टाइम मेड, लाखो की तनख्वा,
कहाँ है वो सुख, वह सूखी रोटी वह हाथ का पंखा।
मेड थी, पर मेरा टिफिन, सुबह उठ ख़ुद ही बना देती
और मेरे लिए चुपड़ी रोटी में एक्स्ट्रा घी भी लगा देती.
माँ तो आख़िर माँ है, उसकी ममता का कोई छोर नहीं,
बस हो गया बहुत, ये शहर, यह नौकरी, अब और नहीं.